FINANCIAL FREEDOM

SIMPLE STEPS TO GETTING OUT OF DEBT

GREGORY DICKOW

Financial Freedom

Unless otherwise noted, all Scripture quotations in this volume are from the *King James Version* of the Bible.

Printed in the United States of America

For information, please write
Gregory Dickow Ministries,
P.O. Box 7000
Chicago, IL 60680

or visit us online at www.changinglives.org.

Table of Contents

FREEDOM FROM DEBT

And Jesus came to Nazareth, where He had been brought up; and, as His custom was, He went into the synagogue on the Sabbath day, and stood up to read. And there was delivered unto Him the book of the prophet Isaiah. And when He had opened the book, He found the place where it was written, "The Spirit of the Lord is upon Me, because He hath anointed Me to preach the gospel to the poor; He hath sent Me to heal the brokenhearted, to preach deliverance to the captives, and recovering of sight to the blind, to set at liberty them that are bruised, to preach [proclaim] the favorable year of the Lord". . . And He began to say unto them, This day is this Scripture fulfilled in your ears."—Luke 4:16-19, 21

God created you to be free from every form of bondage. He sent Jesus, the Anointed One, to remove every burden and destroy every yoke - that includes financial burdens and financial yokes as well. This book will help you to experience that anointing of debt freedom and renew your mind to God's will and His way of thinking concerning finances. By applying the understanding you receive from this material, you can become free from debt forever, beginning today!

Gregory M. Dickow

Get Wisdom

Introduction

"Happy is the man that findeth wisdom, and the man that getteth understanding. For the merchandise of it is better than the merchandise of silver, and the gain thereof than fine gold. She is more precious than rubies: and all the things thou canst desire are not to be compared unto her. Length of days is in her right hand: and in her left hand riches and honour."—*Proverbs 3:13-16*

Wisdom and understanding are the most powerful sources of debt freedom and financial gain. Let's look further at the value of wisdom and understanding described in Proverbs 8:18-19.

"Riches and honour are with me; yea, durable riches and righteousness. My fruit is better than gold, yea, than fine gold; and my revenue than choice silver."

Before going any further, I want to encourage you to ask God for wisdom right now. He said in James 1:5 that when you ask for it, He will give it to you generously. Make this your aim and ambition every day of your life and you will begin to experience more financial freedom than you ever thought possible. Now, let's go on...

In the next few pages, I want to share with you three things:

1. Some of the spiritual laws that guarantee God's abundance for your life.

2. How to experience God's will for your finances.
3. Practical steps to getting out and staying out of debt forever!

Laws That Guarantee God's Abundance

Chapter One

A law is a principle that works the same way every time. A spiritual law is something God has put into *existence*. However, we must put it into *motion* by acting on it—releasing His power into our lives. Allow me to share with you some of the laws of God's abundance that will liberate your finances and your life.

Law #1: The Law of Listening

Listening means hearing God's Word and doing it. In Luke 6:46, Jesus says, "And why do you call me Lord, Lord, and do not do what I say?" To call Jesus "Lord" means to be willing to do whatever He tells us to do. If He is truly the Lord of our lives, then our only response is, "Yes, Lord." If He is the Lord and He says to forgive, you can't say, "No, Lord. I don't want to forgive." Too many Christians make God's Word an option, and, as a result miss out on His blessing for their lives.

“Therefore whosoever heareth these sayings of mine, and doeth them, I will liken him unto a wise man, which built his house upon a rock: And the rain descended, and the floods came, and the winds blew, and beat upon that house; and it fell not; for it was founded upon a rock. And every one that heareth these sayings of mine, and doeth them not, shall be likened unto a foolish man, which built his house upon the sand: And the rain descended, and the floods came,

and the winds blew, and beat upon that house; and it fell: and great was the fall of it."
—*Matthew 7:24-27*

If we want to get out of debt, we must be willing to be obedient to God. In Matthew 7, Jesus equates hearing God's Word and acting upon it with wisdom. Since wisdom produces riches, honor and life, then we should, above all, pursue wisdom. And the clearest definition we have for wisdom is: Hearing God's Word and acting upon it. This is God's system for success. Acting on God's Word works!

Hearing and doing what He says produces supernatural results.

The first recorded miracle Jesus performed took place when they ran out of wine at the wedding of Cana (John 2:1-11). Mary made the most profound statement when she told the servants at the wedding, “Whatever He tells you to do, do it!” (verse 5). The result was the miraculous transformation of water into wine, when they did what He told them to do.

What miracle transformation do you need in your life today? Well, whatever He tells you to do, do it—and you will receive the miracle you need as well!

Law #2: The Law of Honor

The word "honor" means to make heavy, to weigh down, to carry weight. Honor is a lost art in the Body of Christ and in the world. To honor God means that His Word carries so much weight in your life that nothing else anyone says and nothing else happening around you will influence you. Nothing else carries more weight in the decisions you make, the words you speak, the actions you take—than God's Word. That's honor.

For example, let's say you are having financial trouble. Your bills and financial situation are telling you that you don't have enough money to tithe. You are now tempted to honor your circumstances because they are weighing more heavily upon you. To honor

God in that situation means that no matter how heavy and weighty the financial situation is, God's Word carries even more weight than your problem, so you tithe anyway. That honors God. If we only do what He says when it is convenient or when there is no cost, then there is no honor.

This is what Jesus means when He says, "These people honor me with their lips, but their hearts are far from Me" (Matthew 15:8). They were saying, "We honor You, Lord."

But when it came to making decisions, His Word did not "weigh in" heavier than the circumstances they were facing or the opinions they had.

God is our Father and the first commandment with promise according to Ephesians 6:2 is to "Honor your father and mother." In I Samuel 2:30 God says, "Those who honor Me, I will honor." In other words, God is saying, "If My Word carries weight in your life, and you carry it out, your prayers and your words will carry weight in My life and I will carry them out!" What a powerful promise!

With regard to money, honoring God begins by tithing! (Malachi 3:8-11). The tithe is the first tenth of anything you receive. Proverbs 3:9 says, "Honor the Lord with thy substance and with the firstfruits of all thine increase." The result: your barns will be filled with plenty and your vats will overflow with new wine!

Another aspect of honor often overlooked by Christians is the honor that we should regularly show to our spiritual fathers–those who have labored to teach us and establish God's anointing in our lives. These men represent fertile soil suitable for great harvests. We should sow into the soil of their lives if we truly want to experience the anointing that is in their lives. We don't honor with word only, but with our treasure (Matthew 15:8, Matthew 6:21).

Identify the pastor or spiritual father who has made a mark in your life and honor them by sowing into their life. They may not need it, but you need to show it and sow it!

Law #3:
The Law of Seedtime and Harvest

The Bible is not a book of rules, but a bag of seed. Jesus said in Mark 4:26, "The Kingdom of God is like a man who casts seed into the soil." In other words, God's Kingdom is a "system" of sowing and reaping.

This is a universally accepted law that works in every area of life. We reap what we sow. Although this is a concept everyone accepts, it is not a law that everyone follows. Many people try to cheat this system, get around it, or have an unrealistic idea that perhaps today will be different and it won't work.

But it is impossible for this law not to work. God set it into existence in Genesis 8:22–"As long as the earth remains, seedtime and harvest shall not cease."

When we respect this law and decide in advance what kind of harvest we want, then we will act accordingly by planting seeds that are designed by God to produce that harvest. This is God's way—everything He does begins with a seed. Everything we have—good or bad—began with a seed.

Now, you must understand what the Bible is. It is not a book of rules. It is a bag of seed. Every word, every promise written and spoken in the Bible is a seed that when planted in the human heart will produce what God said it will produce.

Our heart and our life are a garden. God formed us out of the soil of the ground according to Genesis 2:7. He designed us to be the soil in which His Word is sown and grown.

If I have a bill I cannot pay, there is a promise in God's Word to cover that. I must reach into the bag of seed (the Bible), pull out the seeds concerning that need (for example—Matthew 6:33, Philippians 4:19, Psalm 34:10, John 15:7), speak that Word out of my mouth, and trust God to bring it to pass. Jeremiah 1:12 (Amp.) says, " . . . He is watching over His Word to perform it." By meditating on these Scriptures, speaking them out of my mouth and listening to anointed teaching of the Word, I am planting and watering the seeds in the soil of my heart. And in due season, I will reap a harvest of God's supply and supernatural provision.

When we combine the sowing of "Word" seeds along with honoring God and sowing "tithes" and "offering" seeds, we are putting ourselves in a position to receive supernatural abundance in our finances, making us ready to get out and stay out of debt forever.

Now let's find out the will of God for our finances and how to experience it...

Experiencing God's Will For Your Finances

Chapter Two

"And be not conformed to this world; but be ye transformed by the renewing of your mind, that ye may prove what is that ***good***, and ***acceptable***, and ***perfect***, will of God." *—Romans 12:2*

The Will of God: 3 Stages of Growth

Notice here that there are three descriptions of the will of God—the good, the acceptable, and the perfect. The Bible reveals a process of three stages of growth in several places.

- I John 2:12-14 shows the 3 stages of spiritual maturity—little children, young men, and fathers.

- Mark 4:20 reveals this in our harvest—30 fold, 60 fold, then 100 fold.
- Mark 4:28 shows the process of a seed's growth—first the blade, then the head, then the mature grain in the head. (NAS).
- In Romans 12:2, we see that process where the will of God is concerned: good, acceptable and perfect.

Let's see how this process relates to our finances:

1. The Good Will of God. Being in the good will of God, financially, means spending less than what you are bringing in. If you are spending more than what you are taking in, you're not in the will of God at all. You're out of the will of God. You do not need more money. In this situation, more money will not solve your problem. You need to spend less than you are taking in. I realize this sounds elementary, but many people are in debt simply because they spend more than what they take in.

2. The Acceptable Will of God. Being in the acceptable will of God, financially, is when your assets are greater than your liabilities. You might say, "I have a mortgage on my house. Am I out of the will of God?" No, this is the acceptable will of God. However, some people have a second and third mortgage on their house, and they end up owing more than the house is actually worth. Many people also owe more on their credit cards than their assets are worth. ***Credit cards are one of the main sources of debt.***

If your assets, including your home and other readily saleable items, are greater than the bills you owe and you are spending less than you are taking in, then you are in the acceptable will of God, and you can ultimately get completely out of debt.

3. The Perfect Will of God. Being in the perfect will of God, financially, means you have all assets with no liabilities. You owe no man anything but to love him (Romans 13:8). Your mortgage is paid off and your credit cards are paid at the end of every month. You're never paying a dollar in interest. You never buy anything with a credit card that you cannot afford. (On this note, it is never right to buy anything with credit cards on the "faith" that the money will come in. That's not faith.

It's foolishness. Wait until the money comes in, then make the purchase.)

It is our desire to come into the perfect will of God in the area of our finances. But you should not be discouraged or condemned if you don't begin there. Start where you're at and begin to experience the progress that will ultimately put you into His perfect will.

Now, how do you make progress to the perfect will of God? Let's look at the verse again—"...Be transformed by the renewing of your mind...that you may do the will of God."

Renew Your Mind. To the degree you submit to the process of renewing your mind, to that degree you will experience the will of God. The more you get your thinking, your words and your decisions in line with God's thinking, God's Words, and God's decisions, the more of God's will you will experience in your life—it's that simple.

The renewing of your mind (meditating on the Word concerning finances, confessing God's Word, changing the way you think, etc.)

will transform your life and your finances. As you wash your mind from wrong ways of thinking and decision making, you will ultimately get into the perfect will of God. As a man thinks, so is he—(Proverbs 23:7).

Many people try to find shortcuts to financial freedom, but as long as your thinking stays the same, your financial situation will stay the same. But as your thinking goes to a higher level (through thinking God's thoughts), it will elevate your finances (and every area of your life for that matter) to a higher level as well. Remember this, following the process of renewing your mind will always produce progress into the perfect will of God.

Next, let's look at some simple steps to get out and stay out of debt forever!

Ten Simple Steps To Get Out Of Debt

Chapter Three

1. Make a decision to not get into any further debt from this moment forward. This foundational decision will guide and govern all smaller decisions concerning your finances. In order to make this decision, you need to understand the problems debt creates in your life:

A. It robs you of your future.

B. It creates an illusion of premature success that is not really there just because you bought something that, in essence, you really don't own.

C. It leaves you powerless over the situation.

D. It forces you to make decisions that you would not have otherwise made.

E. Borrowing breeds more borrowing, disregarding the boundaries of a godly budget.

2. Write down everything you owe and then speak to it as a mountain that must obey you. Command each debt to be removed now, in the Name of Jesus!

> *"For verily I say unto you, that whosoever shall say unto this mountain, be thou removed, and be thou cast into the sea; and shall not doubt in his heart, but shall believe that those things which he saith shall come to pass; he shall have whatsoever he saith. Therefore I*

say unto you, what things soever ye desire, when ye pray, believe that ye receive them, and ye shall have them." —Mark 11:23-24.

This brings God's supernatural power into partnership with the natural steps that you need to take.

3. Reverse the process of what got you there. Make a list of what caused you to get into debt whether it was lust or the need for immediate gratification, or the need to look successful to others, etc. and stop making decisions based on those things.

4. Divide your money up into non-negotiable spending and negotiable spending. For example, tithing is a non-negotiable. Paying your rent is a non-negotiable. After adding up all of the non-negotiables, figure out what is negotiable. This is the only amount that you can ever "play with" or go shopping with, etc. The non-negotiable money must be untouchable to you, even if that includes all of it right now.

ew dress, for example, (whether you believe it or not) is a "negotiable." Going out to eat is a "negotiable." You must be willing to forego the "negotiables" for a season of time.

5. Get control of your spending now. You must spend less than you earn. Create a budget including the simple concept described in #4 and stick to that budget.

6. Deal honestly with your creditors. Don't wait for them to find you. Go to them with a plan, even if it means paying them $25 a month. Most creditors would rather receive something than nothing. And if you go to them, it shows good faith (Matthew 5:25).

7. Pay off debts with the highest interest rate first. Often people take the route of consolidating debts into one. Unfortunately, this eliminates the possibility of rapid debt reduction. Keep your debts separate. Pay them off one at a time. This will eliminate your debt more rapidly and give you a sense of accomplishment along the way.

8. Once you have paid off one debt, use that monthly payment that you were paying to apply toward what you are already paying on the other ones. (Always pay more than the minimum balance or it could take you up to 30 years to pay off a $3,000 credit card bill based on an 18.5% interest rate.)

9. When you have paid off your debts, use the monthly payments you were making to save and invest. This is one of the main ways God blesses His people: through faithful stewardship.

10. Give your way out of debt. If what Jesus said is true, and we know that it is, then we need to apply it to the cancellation of our debt: "Give and it shall be given unto to you; good measure, pressed down, and shaken together, and running over!"—*Luke 6:38*

Your giving must not stop when you are in debt. It actually should increase. Once again, this gets God to partner with you in the process of debt freedom.

Look up the places in Scripture where debt was canceled in the Bible. For example, the widow who met Elijah (I Kings 17:8-16) and the widow who met Elisha (2 Kings 4:1-7).

Know Your Rights and Your Inheritance

Chapter Four

Finally, and most importantly, you must know that it is your right and your inheritance as a child of God to be out of debt and to live debt free. When you aren't sure you have the right to something, you become passive in your pursuit of it. But the righteous are as bold as a lion. You have every right to be financially free!

You are the seed of Abraham (Galatians 3:29) and a joint heir with Jesus Christ (Romans 8:17).

Everything that belongs to Him belongs to you and as He is, so are you in this life (I John 4:17).

Proverbs 13:22 says the wealth of the sinner is laid up for the righteous!

And you are the righteousness of God (2 Corinthians 5:21). Therefore, you have the right to financial freedom!

By making these confessions and combining the spiritual laws in this book with the practical strategies given, your days of financial bondage and debt will come to an end—and you will begin to experience surplus and abundance in every area of your life. ***Start today and never look back!***

Your Declaration of Freedom From Debt

Chapter Five

In the Name of Jesus I believe it is God's will for me to receive all that He wants me to have. I believe God wants me to get out of debt and stay out of debt forever. I believe it is God's will for me to be prosperous. I believe financial freedom means more than just having enough for my needs. It means having enough for my needs and the needs of those around me. God's Word declares that He desires that I prosper and be in health even as my soul prospers. I'm expecting my soul to prosper as I meditate on the Word of God, and that's going to bring prosperity in every other area of my life!

In Jesus' Name, I come against the spirit of debt and the spirit of poverty. I adjure the spirit of debt and the spiritual forces behind it, out of my life, out of my home, out of my family, out of every area of my life. In the Name of Jesus, I command debt to be removed and cast into the sea; and I do not doubt, but I believe that those things which I say shall come to pass. In Jesus' Name, I am expecting the supernatural overflowing abundant provision of God according to His written Word.

In Jesus' Name, Satan, take your hands off of me and my finances. Poverty, get your hands off of me. I have more than enough. I'm not living in the land of just enough anymore. I'm not living in the land of not enough anymore. I step over. I cross over, out of the land of just barely enough and into the land of more than enough. My God shall supply all my needs according to His riches, according to His glory in Christ Jesus. I'm not a victim; I am a victor. I'm the head and I'm not the tail.

In Jesus' Name, I shall lend to many nations, but I shall not borrow. I will have enough for my needs and those around me. My Heavenly Father knows my needs before

I even ask Him. And He supplies my needs according to His riches, not mine, according to His ability, not mine. I receive His ability and release it with my words. I receive complete freedom from debt, and I receive the wisdom of God for my finances and every area of my life in Jesus' Name!

Signature ______________________________

Date ______________________________

Scriptures for Meditation

Genesis 39:2

Father, I thank You that true success and prosperity is: You being with me.

2 Peter 1:3

I thank You that Your "divine power has given me all things that pertain to life and godliness."

2 Corinthians 9:8

And that I "having all sufficiency in everything may have an abundance for every good deed."

3 John 2

I thank you Father that I am prospering and in good health just as my soul is prospering.

Deuteronomy 8:18

Father, I remember today that it is You, the Lord my God who is continually giving me power and ability to get wealth that Your covenant may be confirmed on the earth.

Deuteronomy 28:2

Father, I thank You that all the spiritual and material blessings in Your Word shall come upon me and overtake me because I obey the Lord my God.

Joshua 1:8

I meditate in the Word day and night and I do according to all that is in it, therefore I make my way prosperous and I have great success.

Psalm 112:2-3

Father, I thank You that my descendants will be mighty upon the earth and that I am blessed…I thank you that wealth and riches are in my house and my righteousness endures forever.

Luke 6:38

As I give it is given to me; good measure, pressed down, shaken together and running over, men will pour into my lap.

Proverbs 3:9; 10:4,22; 11:24, 25; 13:21, 22

I honor the Lord from my wealth and from the first of all my produce, and my barns are filled with plenty and my vats are overflowing…I am diligent in all my work and I am made rich…I thank You Father that it is Your blessing that makes me rich and no sorrow comes with it…Father, I thank you that as I scatter I will increase all the more…I am a generous man and I will be prosperous, I water others and I too will be watered…thank You that adversity pursues sinners, but I, a righteous man, am rewarded with prosperity…I call forth the wealth of the sinner into my life, for it is stored up for me…

2 Corinthians 8:9

Jesus, I thank You for your grace, for though you were rich You became poor, that I through Your poverty might become rich.

Psalm 65:11

"Thou hast crowned my year with Your goodness and all of my paths drip with abundance".

About the Author

Gregory Dickow is the host of "Changing Your Life," a dynamic television show seen throughout the world, reaching a potential 450 million households. He is also the founder and Senior Pastor of Life Changers International Church, a diverse and thriving congregation in the Chicago area with several thousand in weekly attendance.

Known for his ability to communicate the power and principles of God's Word clearly and concisely, Pastor Dickow lives to see the lives of people dramatically changed forever.

Pastor Dickow is also founder of Valeo International, a family of churches and ministries committed to spreading the Gospel of Jesus Christ, planting churches, and making disciples around the world.